Cake Decorating
◆ MADE EASY ◆

Cake Decorating
◆ MADE EASY ◆

JUDY KELSEY

THE
APPLE
PRESS

A QUINTET BOOK

Published by The Apple Press
6 Blundell Street
London N7 9BH

ISBN 1-85076-377-1

This book was designed and produced by
Quintet Publishing Limited
6 Blundell Street
London N7 9BH

Creative Director: Richard Dewing
Designer: Nicky Chapman
Project Editor: William Hemsley
Photographer: Trevor Wood

Typeset in Great Britain by
Central Southern Typesetters, Eastbourne
Manufactured in Hong Kong by
Regent Publishing Services Limited
Printed in Hong Kong by
Leefung-Asco Printers Limited

Contents

Introduction

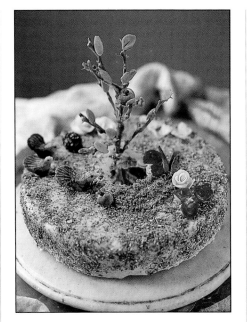

As a child, the first thing I did on my birthday was to come downstairs to see the cake that I knew my mother would have waiting for me on the table. It would be covered with an embroidered lilac throwover, and the whole family would have to be present to witness my delight when the cloth was lifted and my mother's latest creation was revealed. Remembering these cakes now, I see them as tiny works of art: a fairy wood, a field of horses, a ballet class, a gymnasium, the passions of my childhood lovingly depicted on the top of my birthday cake. The pleasure they gave is still with me, although I could not tell you what sort of cake lay under the decoration.

I believe visual pleasure is as necessary for most of us as the need for food and shelter. There is plenty of evidence to suggest that, from cave dwellers to the present day, as human beings we have decorated and adorned ourselves and our surroundings. The quantity and quality of the adornment varies, depending on the materials and tools available, and on the cultural requirements of the society of the time. But adornment is always there.

Today, near the end of the Twentieth Century, most Western cultures are bombarded with visual sensation. Streets lined with hoardings and graffiti are like an ever-present art gallery. The television and the cinema are constant reminders of the wealth of talent our world is filled with. It is easy to feel intimidated by other people's creativity, but the urge to be creative in some form or other lurks in all of us. Making food visually attractive is a satisfying outlet.

This book is not intended as a textbook of "dos and don'ts". I would like it to be a manual of how to go about producing your own ideas. Use it as a springboard for your imagination. Look at the photographs and let your mind take off. I hope it will enable you to spend hours of happy decorating.

Basic Equipment

Bowls

Two or three bowls of various sizes are sufficient for most cakes. Have several small containers to hand if you are making various coloured icings. One medium-sized bowl, preferably with a flattish base, should be able to sit on a pan of hot water if necessary.

Piping bag

A piping bag with a small selection of nozzles, or an icing set, is essential for all but the most basic of decorations. Most icing sets include plain and star-shaped nozzles of various sizes. With good quality sets there are usually extra nozzles that can be bought to use with the plunger.

Palette knife

For easier spreading and a good finish. For cakes where a perfect finish is not required, an old-fashioned kitchen knife with a rounded end will suffice.

Sieve

To sift icing sugar. If the icing sugar has gone very lumpy, you can put it in a food processor to eliminate the lumps, or put it in a strong plastic bag and crunch the lumps out with a rolling pin.

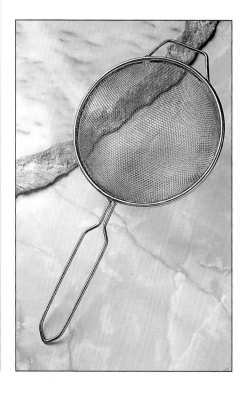

TO MAKE AN ICING BAG OUT OF GREASEPROOF PAPER

1 First make a sheet of greaseproof paper about 12 in/30 cm square by folding a triangle and then cutting with scissors along the attached edge.

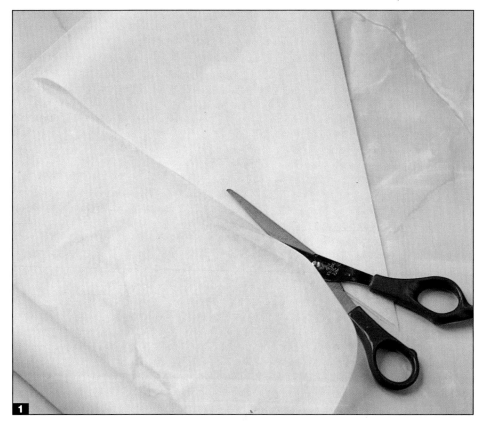

2 3 4 5 Fold the paper three times as shown, ending up with a much smaller triangle.

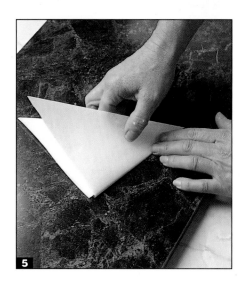

6 Roll up the triangle to form a cone.

7 Fold down the point at the open end of the cone.

8 With scissors, snip across the bottom of the cone to make a hole of the required size.

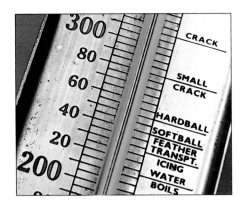

Sugar Thermometer

A sugar thermometer is the simplest and most efficient way to obtain a sugar syrup that is the correct temperature. Have a container filled with hot water to put the thermometer in before you use it, to avoid breakage resulting from sudden heating. Put the thermometer back in the hot water when the syrup is cooked to prevent syrup from drying on. If you do not have a thermometer, use the following chart as a guide.

102°C/215°F Syrup forms fine threads from the end of a spoon.

115°C/240°F Syrup forms a soft ball when dropped into cold water.

120°C/250°F Syrup forms a ball that holds its shape but is still a little soft when dropped into cold water.

140°C/280°F Syrup forms a hard lump when dropped into cold water.

155°C/310°F Syrup breaks like glass when dropped into cold water.

173°C/345°F Syrup starts to change colour.

Colourings

Liquid food colourings are suitable for most icings, but the paste variety is better for moulding icings because they are less likely to upset the consistency of the icing paste. Choose four or five strong, basic colours, and then you can mix them as you would paints. I always mix the colour in an egg-cup and put a few drops onto a sheet of white paper kitchen towel to check the colour before adding it to the icing. To achieve pale colours, dilute with a little water and add to the icing a little at a time until just the right shade is reached.

Paintbrush

Use a fine paintbrush to paint onto icings or moulded decorations.

Greaseproof or silicon paper

Useful for making piping bags, templates or designs to be transferred onto a cake.

Basic Decorating

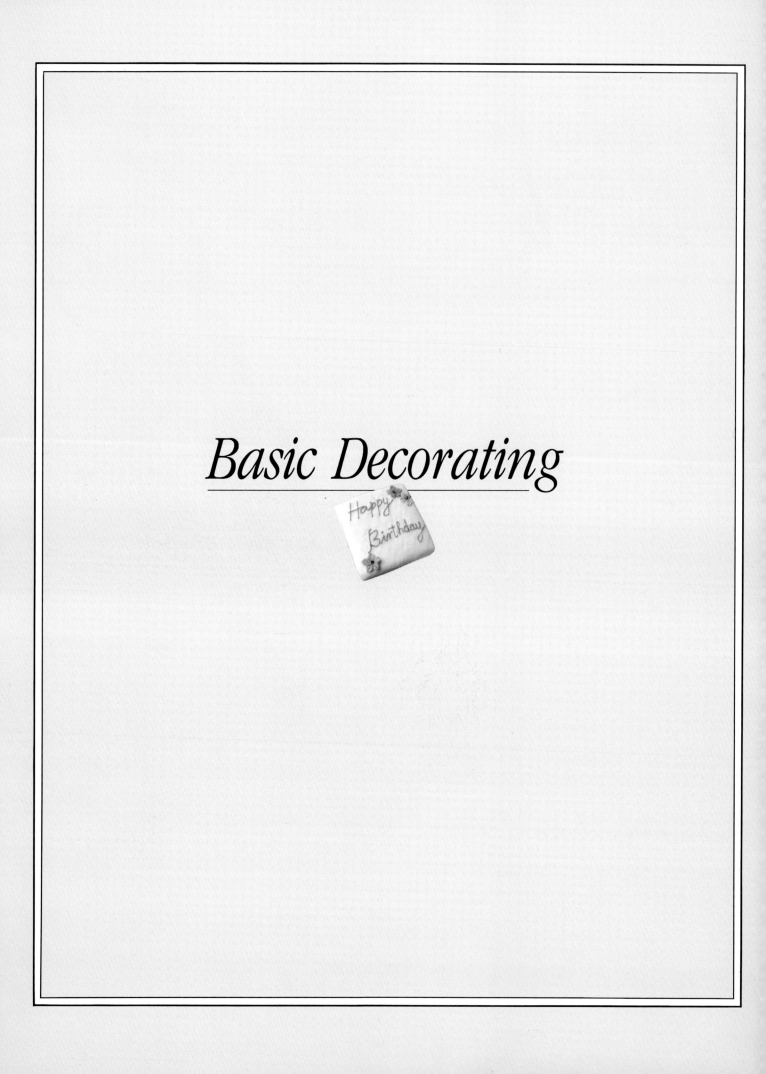

Simple Decorating Techniques

Food that is a pleasure to the eye is always more appetizing than something thrown together with no thought given to its appearance. It is possible to make pretty decorations with nothing more complicated than your normal kitchen utensils: a knife, fork and spoon. If all you have ever done is put nuts and cherries on the top of a cake, it is a good idea to try some of these simple techniques to get the feel of icing and how it behaves, and to learn your own strengths and weaknesses in terms of design. Try these techniques with a butter icing. The joy of butter icing is that if it all goes wrong you can dip the knife in hot water, smooth the icing over and start again.

Decoration using a fork

The illustrations here give only a few examples of the infinite variety of designs you can produce using a fork with butter icing (knife and spoon decorations are illustrated on the next page). You could try the illustrated patterns yourself, or just let your imagination run free!

Decoration using a knife

Decoration using a spoon

Nozzles

Nozzles can be used with all icings that are not meant for moulding. Whenever you are working with nozzles, it is a good idea to have a large plate, marble slab or sheet of grease-proof paper beside you. The flow from a nozzle will vary for all sorts of reasons: the consistency of the icing, the temperature of the icing, the size of the nozzle and the type of icing you are using. Test how the icing is coming out before you apply it to a cake. To obtain a good pattern that keeps its shape, the icing needs to be quite thick, but not so thick that it is not easy to push through a nozzle. Make sure you always have some spare icing sugar to thicken the mixture if necessary. If the mixture is too thick, add water a few drops at a time. Very little moisture is needed to thin down a thick icing. If you are using a fine nozzle, the icing should be freshly made to ensure no dry lumps have formed. If there are lumps, put the mixture through a sieve.

It is possible to make a variety of designs with a few well chosen icing nozzles.

SIZES 1 AND 2

SIZE 5

SIZE 8

SIZE 12

SIZE 14

Feathering

Feathering is a very effective but simple technique. You will need enough icing to cover the cake in a base colour, and a small quantity of the second colour to be piped on. Both colours should be ready before you start, as it will not work well once the icing has begun to set. Tend to make the icing a little on the thin side, and make sure the icing is flowing easily from the piping nozzle.

1 Cover the cake with the base colour.

2 For a round cake, pipe the second colour in even circles around the cake.

3 With a sharp point, draw evenly spaced lines from the edge to the centre of the cake (mark the centre with a tiny dot before you start).

4 For a square cake, pipe the second colour in straight lines, evenly spaced, across the cake. Then, with a sharp point, draw straight parallel lines at right angles to the piping.

TIP

An alternative method for feathering is to paint (rather than pipe) a second colour onto the base icing and proceed as above.

Lettering

Some lucky people can pick up an icing nozzle as they might pick up a pen and draw straight onto the cake. But if you are like me, it is not that easy. The way to ensure tidy words without tears is to proceed as follows.

1 Draw the shape of the cake onto a piece of greaseproof paper, using the cake tin as a guide – then you will be sure that your lettering is the right size to fit the cake.

2 Next, write or print your words onto the paper.

3 When they are right, place the paper gently over the iced cake and prick the shape of the letters onto the cake using a pin.

> **TIP**
>
> Icing can melt with the heat from your hands, so particularly if you are using a soft icing, make holes in the paper before placing it on the cake; then, using as little pressure as possible, mark through the holes.

4 You can then pipe over the pinpricks with confidence.

Icing Recipes

American Frosting

This shiny icing will look good with a minimum of decoration, but make sure you beat it properly in the final stage or it will not hold its shape.

250 g/8 oz granulated sugar

60 ml/4 tbsp water

pinch of cream of tartar

1 egg white

1 Dissolve the sugar in the water in a heavy-based pan over a low heat. Add the cream of tartar and boil the syrup until it reaches 115°C/240°F, which will take about 10 minutes.

21

3 Form patterns or peaks in the icing with a spoon or knife. Additional decorations should be put on before the frosting sets.

2 While the syrup is boiling, beat the egg white until it forms stiff peaks. When the syrup has reached the correct temperature, pour it slowly onto the beaten egg white and continue beating until the mixture holds its shape. Spread the icing quickly over the cake.

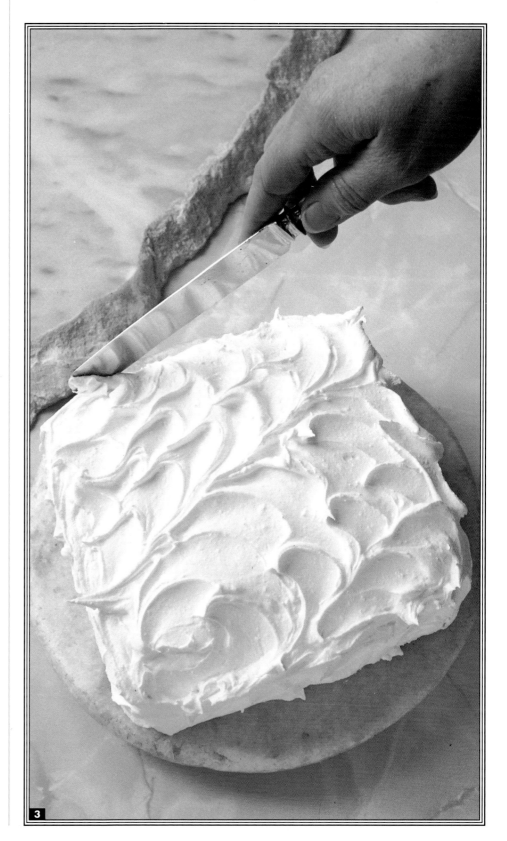

Butter Icing

This standard icing is suitable for most cakes and can be used as a filling if you are making a sandwich cake. For a less rich covering, reduce the amount of butter.

110 g/4 oz butter cut into small knobs

225 g/8 oz sifted icing sugar

45–60 ml/2–3 tbsp boiling water

Place the icing sugar and butter into a bowl. Add the boiling water a little at a time, stirring constantly, until the butter is well blended and a smooth icing is formed. Spread over the cake and smooth with a palette knife. Decorate using a piping nozzle, and add additional decorations if required.

CHOCOLATE BUTTER ICING

Add 10 g/1 tbsp of sifted cocoa powder to the icing sugar, and a few drops of vanilla essence. Decorate with chocolate shapes.

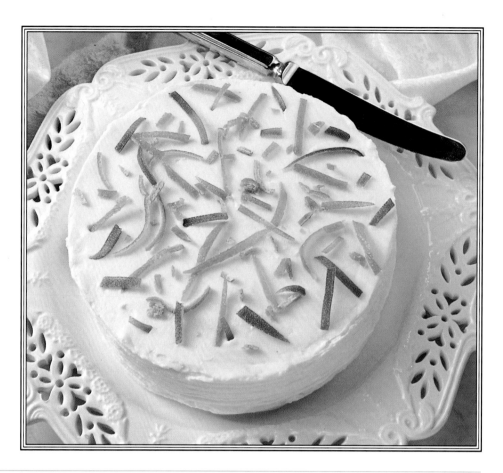

LEMON or ORANGE BUTTER ICING

Replace water with hot lemon or orange juice. Decorate with citrus juliennes (page 38)

COFFEE BUTTER ICING

Dissolve 10 g/1 tbsp of instant coffee in an equal amount of hot water. Add to the icing sugar and butter, with additional hot water as required. A pinch of ground nutmeg or cloves can be added. Decorate with nuts or desiccated coconut.

Crème au Beurre

This is a richer covering than butter icing. Use it on special cakes and flavour it with grated chocolate or your favourite liqueur.

2 egg whites
110 g/4 oz sifted icing sugar
110 g/4 oz unsalted butter

Flavouring
25 g/1 oz grated chocolate or 3 tbsp liqueur

1 Beat the egg whites and the sugar in a bowl over a pan of gently boiling water until they form soft peaks. Beat the butter until it is pale and creamy.

2 Beat in the egg white and sugar mixture a little at a time. Allow to cool.

3 Add grated chocolate, liqueur or other flavouring. Once the icing is on the cake, add decorations if required.

Glacé Icing

Glacé icing is ideal for a smooth finish to a cake and for finely piped decorations.

225 g/8 oz sifted icing sugar

30–45 ml/2–3 tbsp hot water

5 ml/1 tbsp of vanilla or almond essence to flavour

Colouring

1 Put the icing sugar into a bowl. Add the water gradually, mixing all the time, until the mixture is smooth and slightly runny. Add flavouring and colouring if required.

2 For a smooth glossy finish, tip the mixture onto the centre of the cake.

3 Spread a little towards the edges, then gently tilt the cake backwards and forwards until the whole surface is covered. Smooth the mixture over the sides of the cake with a hot palette knife. Leave to dry.

Fudge Icing

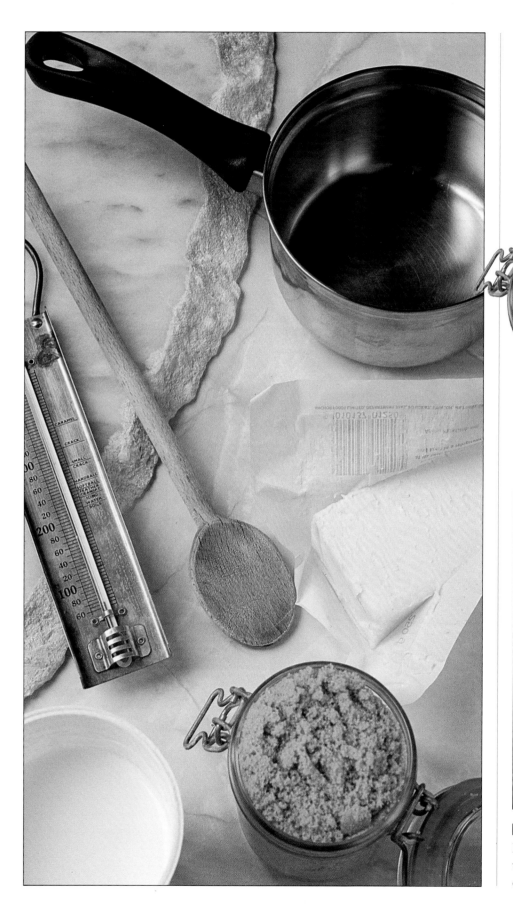

A quick and easy finish for a cake. The crunchy top needs no further decoration. Add 10 g/1 tbsp of cocoa powder to make a chocolate fudge.

49 g/1½ oz butter
110 g/4 oz soft brown sugar
30 ml/2 tbsp single cream

1 Put all the ingredients into a heavy-based pan over a low heat until the butter is melted and the sugar dissolved.

2 Simmer until the mixture leaves the sides of the pan. Be careful not to over-cook because the fudge will then become very hard and start to turn to toffee.

3 When cooked, spread quickly over the warm cake.

Royal Icing

Royal icing is the traditional icing to use on fruit cakes for special occasions, such as weddings, christenings or anniversaries The cake needs careful preparation before the royal icing is applied (see Christmas Fruit Cake, page 63).

700 g/1½ lb sifted icing sugar
2½ ml/½ tsp cream of tartar
3 egg whites
5 ml/1 tsp vanilla essence

1 Place the sifted icing sugar in a bowl with the cream of tartar. In another bowl, whisk the egg whites until they are foamy but not stiff.

2 Stir the egg whites into the sugar, add the vanilla essence and then beat until the icing is smooth. Add more icing sugar if the mixture is too thin.

3 Secure the prepared cake onto a cake board using a little of the icing. Spread the icing over the cake with a palette knife. (If you have an icing ruler, make a professional finish by pulling the ruler at a 45° angle towards you, working from side to side with a fluid motion.) Trim the edges and leave for the icing to dry.

4 To ice the sides, spread the icing on evenly with a palette knife. Finish with an icing scraper if you have one. A wide variety of decorations may be added, such as the piped icing and moulding-icing flowers illustrated here.

Fondant Icing

Fondant icing is more time consuming to prepare than the other icings in this chapter, but once it is made you can keep it well-wrapped in the refrigerator for several months to use as you require it. I give two methods of making it: use whichever one suits you best.

500 g/1 lb icing sugar

140 ml/5 fl oz water

5 ml/½ tsp vanilla essence or lemon juice

METHOD 1

 Place the icing sugar and the water, and vanilla essence or lemon juice in a heavy-based pan and stir over a low heat until the sugar has dissolved. Bring to the boil until the syrup reaches 115°C/240°F on a sugar thermometer.

2 Pour the hot syrup onto a cold wet working surface or marble board, and leave to cool slightly.

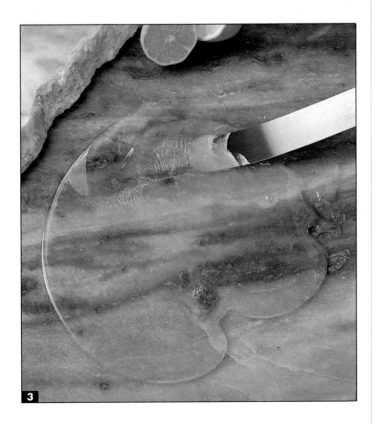

3 Lift the edges of the syrup with a metal spatula and fold towards the centre.

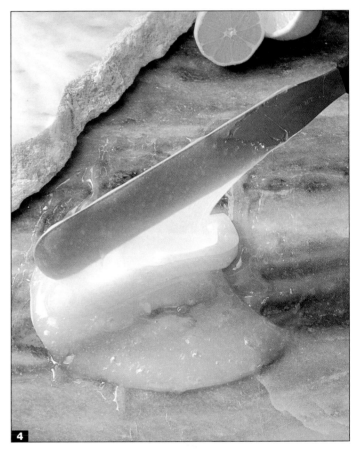

4 Continue working round the syrup with the spatula until the mixture changes from a syrup to dense mass.

5 By this stage it should then be cool enough to handle. Knead with your hands, as if you were kneading dough, until you have a smooth white paste. Wrap and leave to cool completely before storing in the refrigerator.

To use, break off a piece of the required size, place in a bowl over a pan of hot water, and heat gently until the mixture is the consistency of thick cream. You may need to add a little water. You can use the flavourings employed in previous recipes. Use fondant icing in the same way as glacé icing.

METHOD 2

Heat and cook the icing sugar and water as above, then pour one third into a bowl and the remaining two thirds into a larger bowl. With a wooden spoon, beat the mixture until it changes consistency, starting with the smaller amount. When they are both white and thick, tip onto a cold, wet surface, combine the two and knead as above.

Decorations

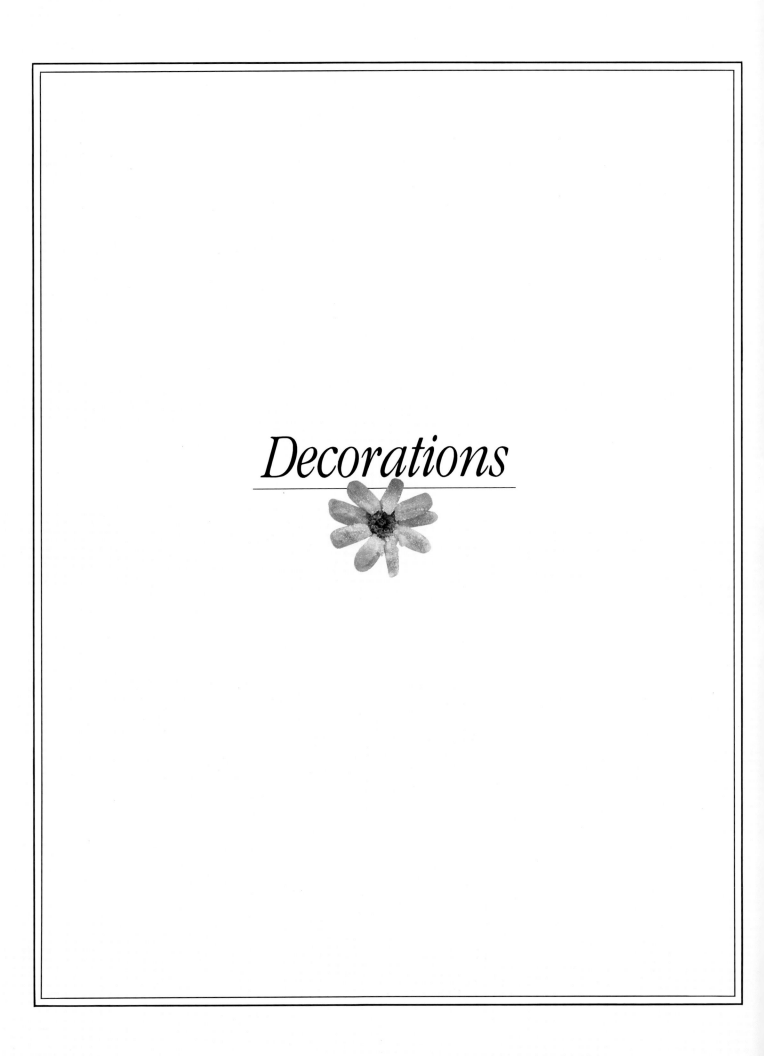

The decorations on a cake should be an integral part of the whole; something that will not only make the cake look more appetizing, but blend naturally with the cake ingredients to add to the taste.

Nuts and crystallized fruits provide a welcome contrast of texture and taste, especially on top of a sweet creamy icing. If there are already nuts or fruits in the cake, make sure you pick out the best formed ones to put on the top of the cake. When you are buying, shop carefully. Choose fresh ingredients, not ones that have sat on the shelf for weeks. It is often possible to tell how fresh an item is simply by looking, and if its wrapped, check the date on the packet. Fresh fruit should be firm and without bruises; crystallized fruits should have kept their colour, and the sugar should be glazed, not white and powdery.

Nuts should look fresh, and not be starting to shrivel and dry out. Whole nuts retain their oils, and consequently their flavour, better than chopped nuts. Almond skins can be easily removed by pouring boiling water over the nuts and leaving for ten minutes. Take the nuts out of the water a few at a time, rub the skin between your fingers and thumb to loosen it, then pop the nut out.

It is worthwhile preparing decorations in advance. The following decorations take a little time, but the effort involved is amply repaid by the results.

Caramelized Nuts

75 g/3 oz granulated sugar
75 ml/3 fl oz water
Nuts (can be roasted lightly in the oven for additional taste)

Dissolve the sugar and water in a heavy-based pan over a low heat. Continue to heat until mixture starts to change colour (at this stage it becomes caramelized). Toss the nuts in the caramel, making sure they are all properly covered. Take the pan off the heat. Remove nuts with a slotted spoon and spread on a baking tray or silicone paper to dry.

Citrus Juliennes

Citrus fruit: oranges, lemons, limes, or a
combination of all three.
75 g/3 oz granulated sugar

1 With a sharp knife, cut the fruit into quarters. Pare away each section of the skin from the fruit, making sure there is no pith left on the skin. Place skin sections on a chopping board and slice carefully into thin matchsticks.

2 Put enough water in a small pan to amply cover the matchstick pieces and bring to the boil for one minute. Drain, then repeat three or four times to get rid of any bitterness.

3 Put the sugar and 150 ml/6 fl oz of water in the pan, dissolve over a low heat, add the juliennes and simmer until they become transparent. Lift out with a slotted spoon.

4 Drain the juliennes on greaseproof or silicone paper.

·Crystallized Flowers

I love to do this. The flowers look so pretty that I am often reluctant to use them. I have kept primroses preserved in gum arabic for over a year, but store them very carefully or they will break.

GUM ARABIC RECIPE
25 g/1 oz gum arabic crystals
60 ml/4 tbsp rose flower water
Caster sugar
Fresh edible flowers or leaves

2 Hold a flower (or leaf) by the stem and carefully paint all over with the gum arabic mixture.

1 Place the gum arabic and the rosewater in a screwtop jar and leave for two or three days for the gum arabic to dissolve. A warm airing cupboard is ideal. When the crystals have dissolved, prepare a shallow bowl filled with caster sugar, a clean fine paintbrush and a sheet of greaseproof or silicone paper.

3 Place the wet flower, top side down, gently on the caster sugar, making sure that none of the petals have curled under, then sprinkle the underside of the flower with sugar.

4 Lift the flower out of the sugar and place it on the sheet of paper to dry. Leave for 3 or 4 days until the flowers are completely dry, cut off the stems. Store in an airtight container.

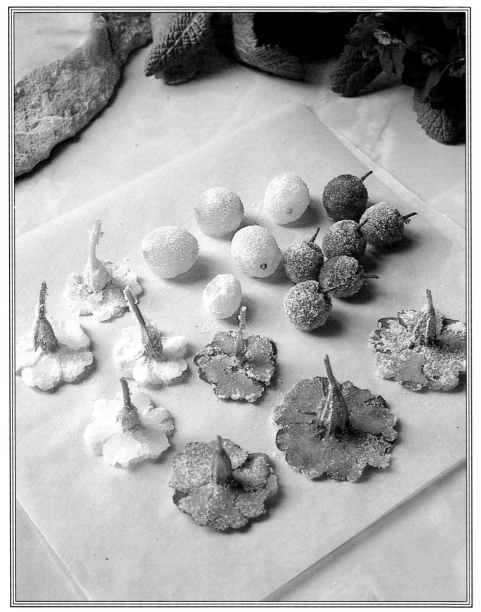

EGG WHITE RECIPE

This recipe is suitable for edible flowers, leaves and soft fruit, but the fruit will not keep for longer than a few days.

Egg white, lightly beaten
Caster sugar
Fresh soft fruit, flowers or leaves

Proceed as above, using egg white instead of the gum arabic mixture.

Glazing

225 g/½ lb apricot jam or red currant jelly
45 ml/3 tbsp water

Heat the jam and the water in a heavy-based pan and stir to dissolve. Boil for 3 or 4 minutes until the mixture thickens. Strain through a sieve and use while still warm. Alternatively, cool and store in an airtight jar and reheat to use.

Templates and Run-outs

Templates are an easy way to produce exactly the shape you want. To make a template, draw or trace your required shape onto a piece of greaseproof or silicone paper. Cut out the shape, place it on your icing, then cut round the shape with a sharp knife.

A run-out is a method of making decorations using glacé, fondant or royal icing. It involves making an outline shape with icing and then flooding it. This can be done directly onto the base icing, or onto a sheet of greaseproof or silicone paper and left to harden before you transfer it onto the cake. The flooding icing needs to be thin and you may need to ease it into the corners with the sharp point of a knife.

BUTTERFLIES

1 Draw the wings, body and antennae onto silicone paper.

2 Using a piping nozzle, draw over the outlines of the shapes.

3 Again using a piping nozzle, flood the shapes.

4 Leave to dry. When the icing is hard, lift carefully off the silicone paper and stick together with a little more icing.

PARROT

Trace a parrot onto a sheet of paper. Using a piping nozzle and white icing, outline the shape, then flood it. When the icing is dry, paint the parrot in bright colours using food colouring.

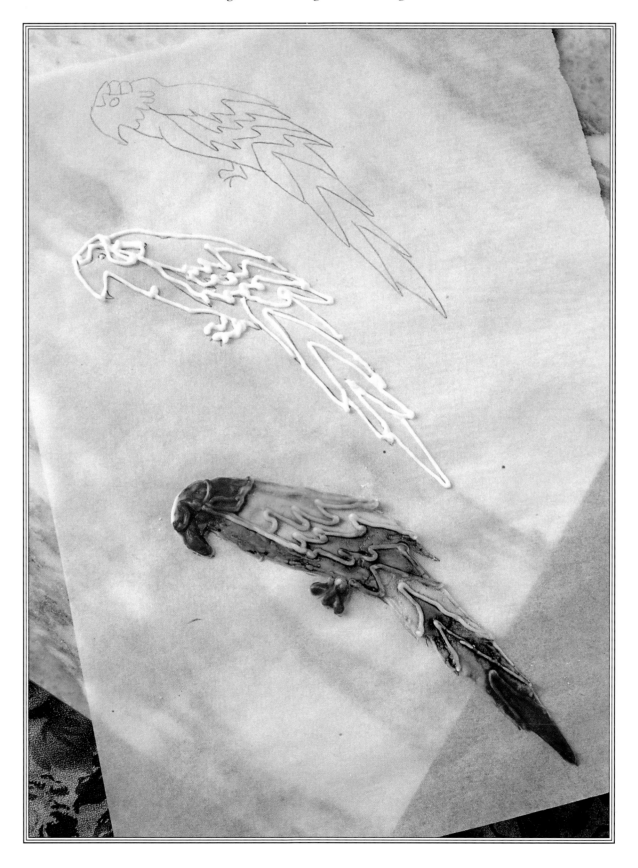

FISH

Draw a fish onto a sheet of paper. Using coloured icing and a plain piping nozzle, outline the fish. To make the fins, draw lines close together with the piping nozzle. Flood the main body of the fish.

TIP

It is often difficult to keep a steady hand when piping. Try keeping your elbow pressed against your body. The support it gives will help to keep your hand steady

Chocolate

Chocolate decorations are attractive and easy to make. You can use ordinary chocolate or one of the special cooking chocolates available in many shops and most supermarkets.

To melt chocolate, break it into small pieces and place it in a bowl over a pan of hot water. Keep the water simmering gently while the chocolate melts, taking care not to let any water into the bowl.

CHOCOLATE LEAVES

1 Use real leaves as templates – ones with a shiny surface are best.

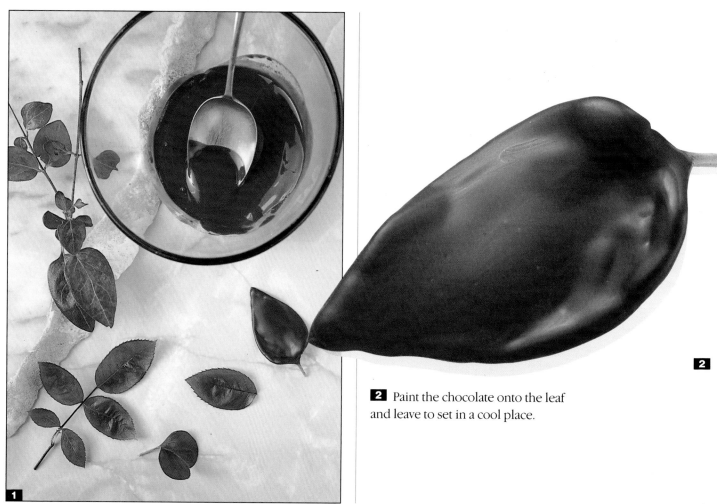

2 Paint the chocolate onto the leaf and leave to set in a cool place.

3 When the chocolate is set, gently peel it off the leaf.

CHOCOLATE SHAPES

1 Pour melted chocolate onto a piece of greaseproof or silicone paper and spread it out evenly with a palette knife.

2 When the chocolate is nearly set, cut out your shapes using a sharp knife.

3 Shapes can be marked out before cutting using a blunt point.

4 Complex shapes, such as these flowers, can be assembled from a number of parts.

5

CHOCOLATE SHREDS
Grate chocolate to make chocolate shreds. Experiment with the different cutters on your grater.

TIP

Melted chocolate can be piped directly onto the cake using a plain nozzle (it does not hold its shape if you use a fancy nozzle) but you must have a sure hand because it is very runny.

5 If you are making a complicated shape from a single piece of chocolate, it is always best to cut it out using a template (see page 42).

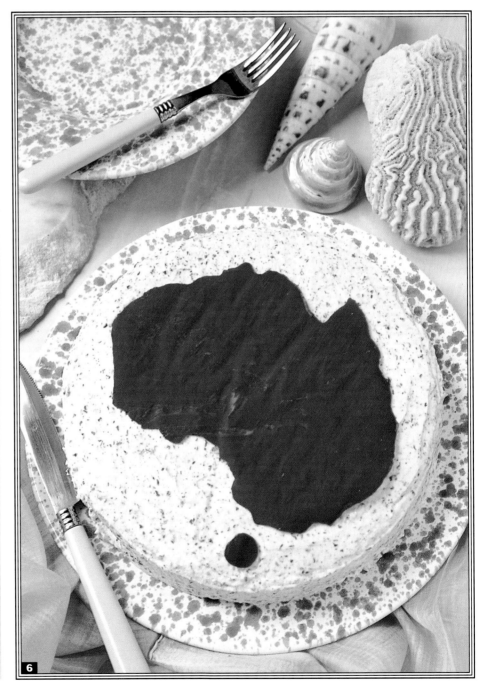

6

6 This chocolate map of Australia sits on a sea of icing sprinkled with chocolate shreds.

Moulding Icings

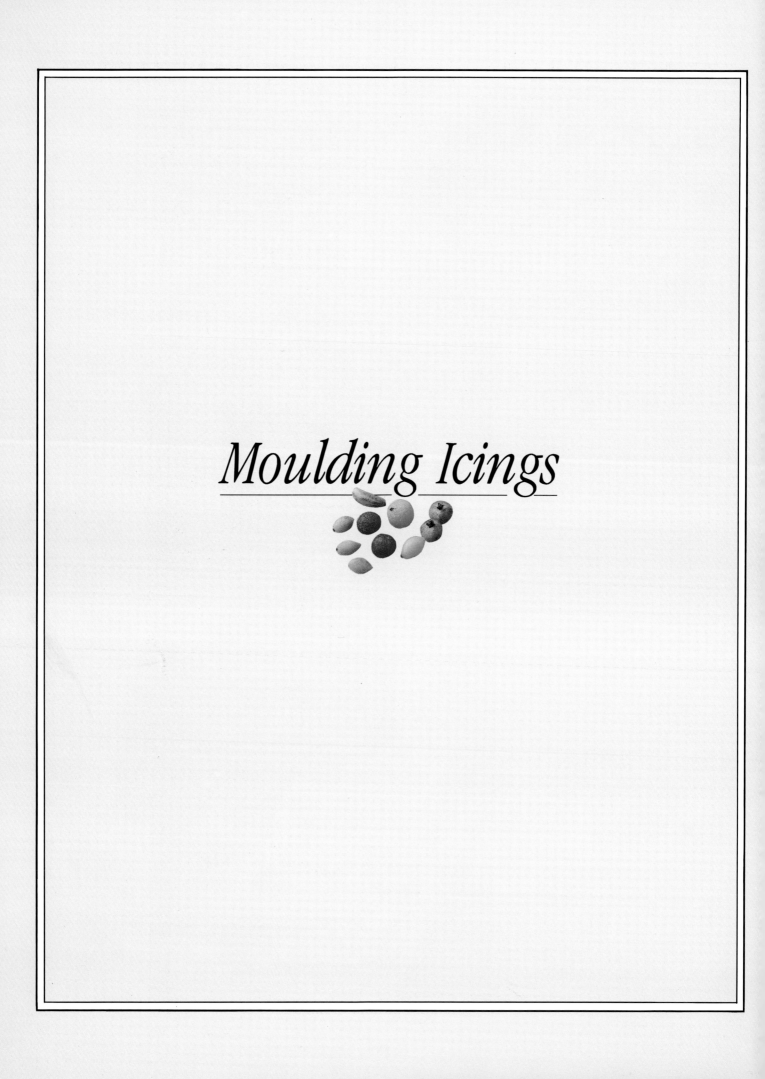

he uses of moulding icings are as varied as nature itself. I recently attended two weddings. At the first, the wedding cake was decorated with exquisite bouquets of icing flowers, perfect in every detail; at the second, the wedding cake was a tableaux of large, jolly, red marzipan bears. Both cakes were equally admired.

The two recipes below can both be used to make cake decorations, or they may be rolled out and used to cover a whole cake. The moulding icing is more maleable than the almond paste, so use it for fine intricate decorations. Almond paste has a more solid consistency and is suitable for larger, bolder shapes.

Specialist shops stock a large variety of modelling tools and fancy cutters to use with moulding icings, which you may like to try. But the ideas below are very simple and do not need implements other than the basic equipment listed at the beginning of the book.

MOULDING-ICING FLOWERS

Moulding Icing

1 egg white
30 ml/2 tbsp liquid glucose
450 g/1 lb icing sugar

Moulding icing is available ready-made at some shops and supermarkets.

TIP

Moulding icing will take the heat from your hands as you work and become less manageable, so try to keep your hands cool and work on a cold surface.

A CAKE DECORATED WITH MOULDING-ICING POPPIES

1 Put the egg white and glucose in a bowl and beat to combine.

2 Add the sugar a little at a time, continuing to stir, until you achieve a stiff paste.

3 Place on a board sprinkled with cornflour and knead until you have a maleable ball. Wrap immediately to prevent drying.

If you are using the icing for decorations, break off a small quantity at a time and keep the rest wrapped up. Colour as desired with paste colouring, or paint with food colouring.

ROSES

LILIES

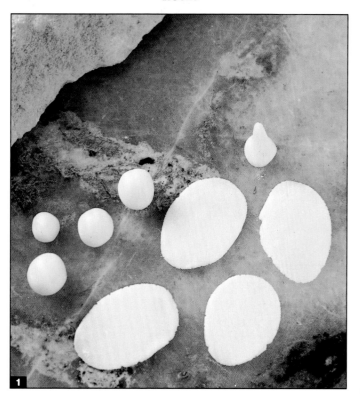

1 Colour the dough suitably with a paste colour. Break off small pieces of dough and roll into balls in the palms of your hands. Roll into thin oblongs.

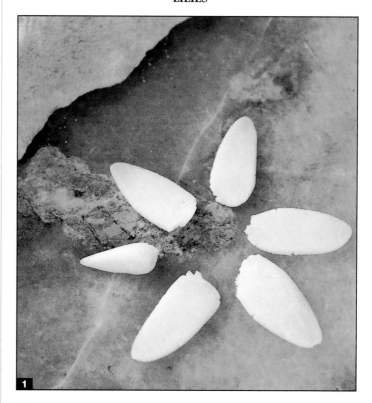

1 Break off small pieces of dough, make into thin cones and then roll out.

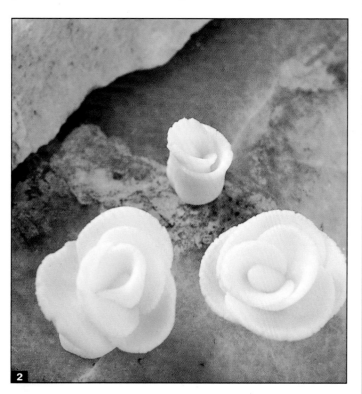

2 Make a slender cone and wrap petals around the cone until you have a rose. Leave to dry and then break off the bottom of the cone.

2 Make a slender cone and wrap the petals around it. Using a fine paintbrush, paint stamens in the centre with food colouring.

POPPIES

1 Colour the dough with bright red paste. Make balls out of the dough and roll out thinly into petals.

2 Attach the petals to a flat ball. The centre can be made out of black moulding icing or painted black. Using a skewer, the wrong end of a fine paintbrush or a similar object, ease up the edges of the petals to produce a wavy effect.

LEAVES

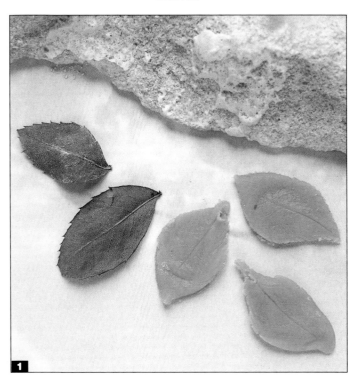

1 Colour the moulding icing green. To use a real leaf as a template, roll out the dough, then press the leaf into it. Using a sharp knife, cut around the edge of the leaf and then lift the leaf off.

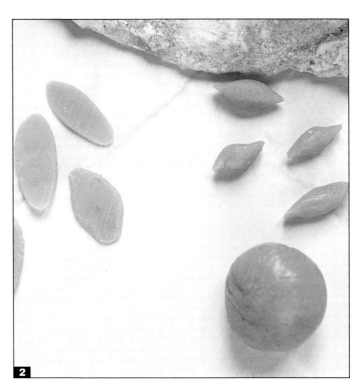

2 Alternatively, you can roll the dough into small sausage shapes with painted ends then press flat with a rolling pin.

Almond Paste

225 g/8 oz ground almonds
225 g/8 oz sifted icing sugar
1 egg, lightly beaten
5 ml/1 tsp lemon juice or orange flower water

1 Combine the ground almonds and icing sugar in a bowl. Add the lightly beaten egg and lemon juice or orange flower water, and mix in with a wooden spoon.

2 Knead into a smooth dough. Wrap and keep in a cool place.

BIRDS

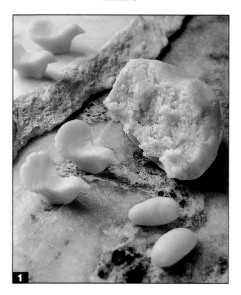

1 Using the palms of your hands, shape a short sausage out of a piece of dough, then squeeze to shape the head and tail. Press the tail into a fan shape using your thumb and forefinger.

2 Paint the almond-paste birds with food colouring.

FRUITS

FANCY SHAPES
To create fancy shapes, dust a clean, dry surface with cornflour or icing sugar and roll out the dough. Cut out shapes using cutters or templates (see page 42).

1 Make the paste into fruit shapes. Whole cloves may be used to represent a stalk. Roll citrus fruit shapes over the fine cutting edge of a grater to achieve a pitted finish.

2 Colour the fruits appropriately by painting with food colouring.

Cake Recipes

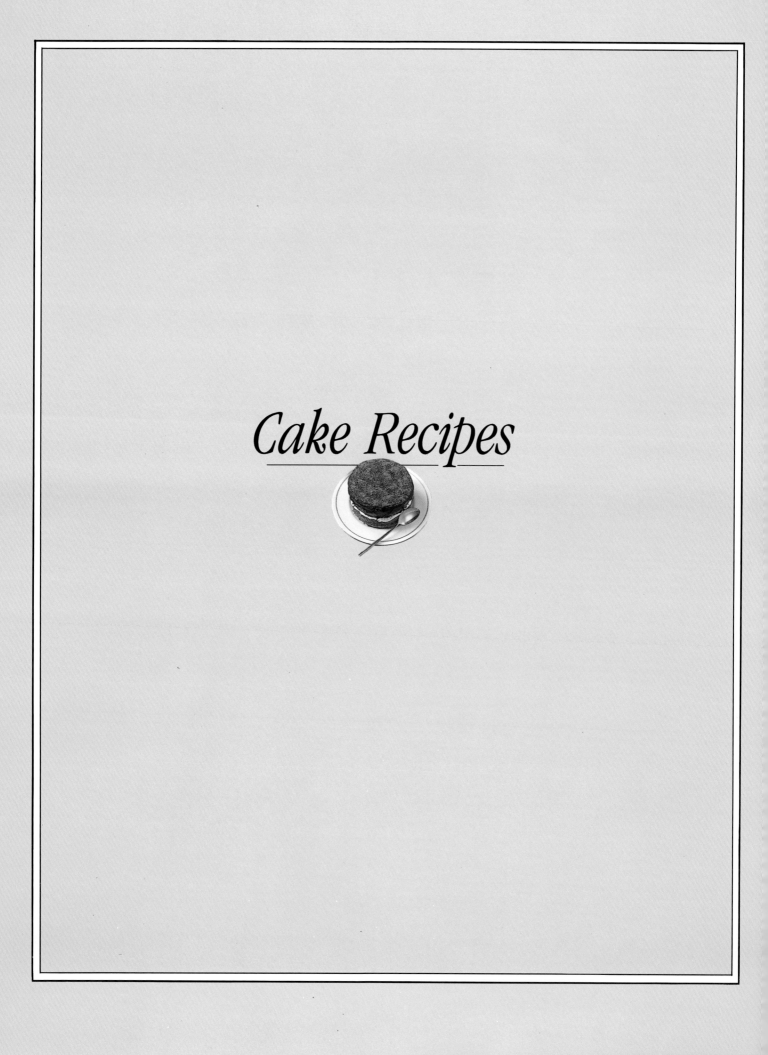

Almond and Hazelnut Cake

This is a delicious cake using ground nuts instead of flour to give a wonderful flavour.

4 eggs
175 g/6 oz sugar
225 g/8 oz ground almonds
225 g/8 oz ground hazelnuts
10 g/2 tsp baking powder
Pinch of salt

Icing
Crème au beurre (page 25)

Decoration
Toasted almond halves
Thin slices of crystallized ginger

Separate the whites and yolks of the eggs. Beat the yolks with the sugar until they are pale and creamy. Mix the ground nuts, baking powder and salt into the sugar mixture.

In a separate bowl, beat the egg whites until they stand in stiff peaks, then fold into the nut mixture.

Bake in two 18 cm/7 in sandwich tins at 180°C/350°F/gas mark 4 for 30–35 minutes. When cooked, turn onto a wire rack to cool.

Fill and ice with crème au beurre. Decorate with toasted almond halves and crystallized ginger.

Apricot Velvet Cake

I used to make this cake with dried apricots or prunes soaked overnight to yield a tasty liquid. Recently, I have been buying the succulent ready-to-eat dried fruit and using orange juice to make up the liquid.

110 g/4 oz butter
110 g/4 oz soft brown sugar
225 g/8 oz sifted self-raising flour
3 eggs, separated
110 g/4 oz finely chopped dried apricots
150 ml/6 fl oz apricot or orange juice

Icing
Butter icing (page 23) with 1 tbsp brandy
(optional)

Decoration
Crystallized fruits

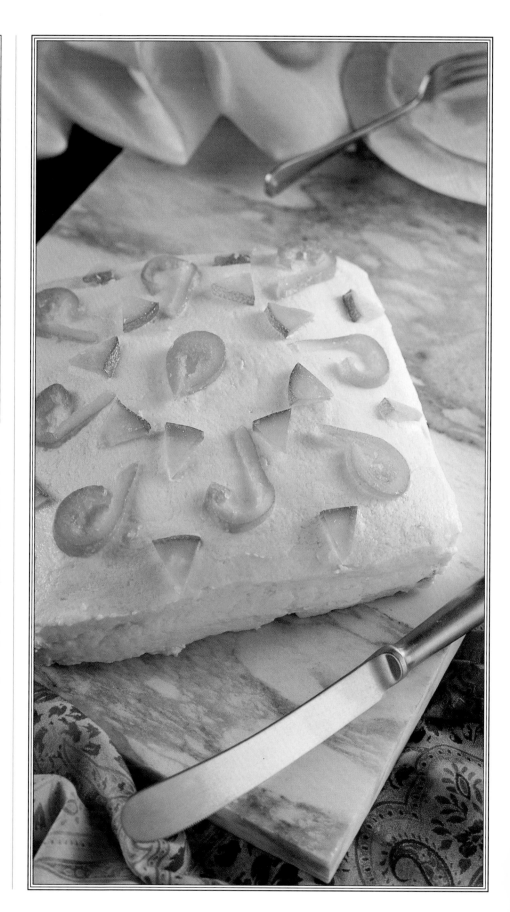

Cream the butter and sugar. Add 1 teaspoon of the flour and then the egg yolks and beat until the mixture is pale and creamy. Add ⅓ of the sifted flour, followed by ⅓ of the juice and mix. Repeat until all the flour and the juice are combined with the butter mixture. Then add the chopped fruit.

Beat the egg whites until they are stiff, then fold them into the cake mixture. Bake in a 20 cm/8 in square tin at 190°C/375°F/gas mark 5 for 1–1½ hours.

Ice with butter icing and decorate with crystallized fruit.

Basic Blender Cake

I love this cake. It has a wonderful soft texture and is very quick to make. A blender is not essential; an egg beater produces the same results, but will take longer. Add nuts to the fudge icing and no further decoration is needed.

2 eggs
110 g/4 oz sugar
8 ml/1 tsp vanilla essence
110 g/4 oz flour
5 g/1 tsp baking powder
pinch of salt
150 ml/6 fl oz milk
10 g/½ oz butter

Icing
Fudge icing (page 28)

Decoration
50 g/2 oz coarsely chopped nuts

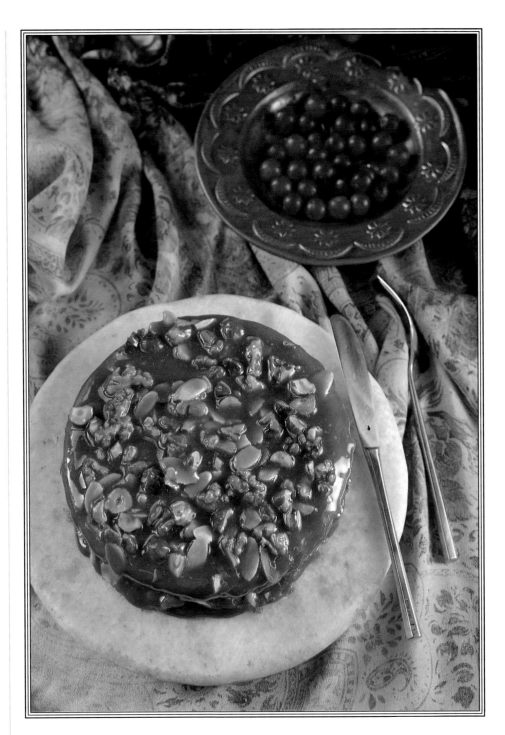

Break the eggs into a blender, food processor or bowl and beat well; add the sugar and vanilla and beat again.

In a small pan, heat the milk and butter to boiling point. Add the flour, baking powder and salt to the egg and sugar mixture, then pour in the milk and beat well. The batter will be thin but do not add any more flour.

Pour the mixture into a 18 cm/7 in round tin and bake at 190°C/375°F/gas mark 5 for 30 minutes.

While the cake is baking, make the fudge icing, adding the nuts. Keep warm over a pan of hot water until the cake is cooked.

Turn the cake onto a wire rack, and while it is still warm spread the fudge icing over the bottom (which then becomes the top) of the cake. Put under the grill for 3–4 minutes to brown lightly.

Chocolate Cake

The secret of this cake is in the beating so do not stint on this part of the recipe. Filled with fresh whipped cream, it is not the sort of cake that will stay in the tin for days.

4 eggs
150 g/5 oz sugar
50 g/6 tbsp flour
20 g/2 tbsp cocoa
20 g/2 tbsp arrowroot

10 g/2 tsp baking powder
8 ml/1 tsp vanilla essence

Filling
175 g/6 oz double or whipping cream

Icing
75 g/3 oz plain chocolate
25 g/1 oz unsalted butter
30 ml/1 tbsp water
75 g/3 oz icing sugar

Beat the eggs until they are frothy, then slowly beat in the sugar until the mixture is really thick and creamy.

Sift the flour, cocoa, arrowroot and baking powder together, then add to the egg and sugar mixture, folding in gently with as little stirring as possible to retain the air. Check that there is no pocket of liquid in the bottom of the bowl. Add the vanilla essence.

Bake in 2 deep 18 cm/7 in sandwich tins at 200°C/400°F/gas mark 6 for 25 minutes. Remove from the tins and cool.

Melt the chocolate in a bowl over a pan of simmering water. Add the butter in small knobs and stir in the icing sugar. Continue stirring until the mixture is smooth. Take off the heat and stir in the water, allow to cool a little and then spread over the top of one of the cakes before it sets.

Spread the whipped cream over the top of the other cake. Sandwich the cakes together with the cream as filling. Sprinkle with finely grated chocolate.

Christmas Fruit Cake

Christmas cakes are usually covered with royal icing (page 30) but I prefer something a bit softer. The icing I use is really a combination of royal and butter icing (page 23). It is not as brittle as royal icing and still lasts well. In the traditional way, I use almond paste as an inner layer of icing.

Christmas Fruit Cake

225 g/8 oz plain white flour

5 g/1 tsp cinnamon

5 g/1 tsp ginger

5 g/1 tsp mixed spice

2 g/½ tsp ground cloves

2 g/½ tsp grated nutmeg

50 g/2 oz ground almonds

225 g/8 oz butter

225 g/8 oz brown sugar

4 eggs

350 g/12 oz sultanas

350 g/12 oz currants

110 g/4 oz seedless raisins

110 g/4 oz chopped mixed peel

110 g/4 oz washed glace cherries,
halved or quartered

50 g/2 oz chopped blanched almonds

100 ml/4 fl oz sherry or milk

80 ml/2 tbsp brandy (optional)

Icing

450 g/1 lb almond paste

1 egg lightly beaten or apricot glaze (page 41)
to cover cake

450 g/1 lb icing sugar

1 egg white, lightly beaten

60 ml/2 tbsp hot lemon juice

50 g/2 oz butter

2–3 tbsp hot water

Decoration

Holly leaves made of almond paste or angelica

Crystallized cherries, halved

Silver or gold balls

Line a 20cm/8 in round cake with a double thickness of greased silicone or greaseproof paper. Prepare the fruit by tossing it in a little of the flour (this prevents it from sinking to the bottom of the cake). Sift the rest of the flour and the spices into a bowl.

Cream the butter and sugar in a large bowl. Add 1 tsp of flour then beat in one egg; repeat 3 times. Gently mix in the rest of the flour, then add the fruit and nuts. Mix in the sherry or milk, adding a little more if the mixture seems dry. Spoon the mixture into the prepared cake tin and smooth across the top with the back of a metal spoon, leaving the sides slightly higher than the centre of the cake.

Bake for one hour at 170°C/335°F/gas mark 3. Lower heat to 150°C/310°F/gas mark 2 and bake for a further hour. Lower heat again 145°C/290°F/gas mark 1 and bake for a third hour. If the cake shows signs of browning too much before it has finished cooking, cover the top loosely with a piece of tinfoil. Test with a fine skewer to make sure the cake is cooked right through.

Allow to cool a little, then add the brandy by pricking the top with a fine skewer and slowly pouring the brandy onto the cake.

When the cake is cool remove it from the tin, leaving the lining paper around it to prevent it from drying out until you are ready to use the cake.

TO ICE THE CAKE

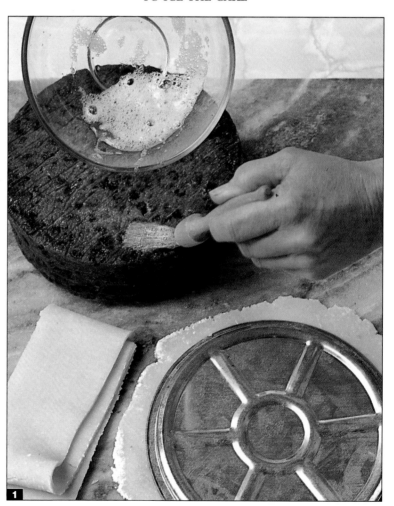

1 Remove the lining paper from around the cake. Cover the cake with apricot glaze or the lightly beaten white of an egg.

2 Dust a clean dry surface with cornflour or icing sugar. Roll out the almond paste. Using the cake tin as a guide, cut out a circle large enough to cover the top of the cake and fold over the side by about 1cm/½ in.

3 Place it on the top of the cake and gently press down the edge onto the side of the cake.

4 Cut a strip of almond icing as wide as the cake is high and long enough to circle the cake. Brush the overlapping edge of the paste on the cake with egg white or apricot glaze, then wrap the long piece of almond paste around the cake. Join the ends with apricot glaze or egg white.

5 To make the icing, first sift the icing sugar. Then break the butter into knobs and blend it into the icing sugar with the hot lemon juice. Add the egg white and sufficient water to mix to a smooth consistency. Spread over the top and sides of the cake.

Decorate with holly leaves made of green-coloured almond paste or angelica, halved crystallized cherries and silver or gold balls.

Butter Sponge

This is one of the first cakes I made as a child, and I have been using the same recipe with its many variations ever since. Below are three of these variations, decorated to turn them into cakes that are a little bit special.

175 g/6 oz self-raising flour

25 g/3 tbsp cornflour

pinch of salt

225 g/8 oz sugar

75 g/3 oz butter

55 ml/2 fl oz milk

5 ml/1 tsp golden syrup

5 ml/1 tsp vanilla essence

3 eggs

LEMON BUTTER SPONGE

Replace the milk with 55 ml/2 fl oz lemon juice, and add the finely grated zest of a lemon to the cake mixture. Add 20 ml/ 1 tbsp of lemon juice to the butter cream filling.

Ice with pale yellow glace icing (page 27) and decorate with crystallized flowers (page 40).

Sift the flour, cornflour and salt into a bowl, and add the sugar. In a small pan, melt the butter. Take off the heat and add the milk, golden syrup and vanilla essence. Stir until the syrup dissolves. Pour the milk mixture onto the flour and sugar mixture and stir to combine.

Add the eggs one at a time, beating well between each egg.

Pour the mixture into two 18cm/7 in well-greased sandwich tins, and bake at 190°C/375°F/gas mark 5 for 25 minutes, or in a 20cm/8 in square tin for 40 minutes.

ROSE BUTTER SPONGE

Replace the water with rose flower water, and add a few drops of pink food colouring to the cake mixture. Bake in a heart shaped tin.

Ice with pale pink glace icing (page 27) flavoured with 5 ml/1 tsp of rose flower water, and decorate with pink roses that have been made with moulding icing (page 52).

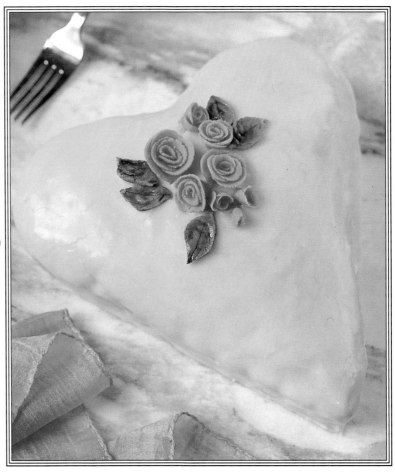

SPICE BUTTER SPONGE

Make this for an Easter or Harvest cake. Add 5 g/½ tsp cinnamon, 5 g/½ tsp ground ginger, and 5 g/½ tsp grated nutmeg to the sifted flour. Bake in a 20 cm/8 in square tin. When the cake is cool slice it in half horizontally.

Add a large knob of butter and ¼ tsp cinnamon to plain glacé icing (page 27). Fill and ice the cake.

To make an Easter cake, make a nest on top of the cake with citrus juliennes and fill with painted almond paste eggs (page 56).

Pavlova Cake

Pavlova Cake

Pavlova Cake was named after the beautiful Russian dancer Anna Pavlova, presumably as a tribute to her lightness and grace. When I was growing up in New Zealand, no special occasion was complete without a "Pav". The soft meringue covered in cream and topped with fruit is the sort of cake that even people who never eat anything sweet will happily consume – and probably come back for a second slice! The recipe is very simple, but two things to remember are that the egg whites must be very stiff if the cake is to retain its shape, and it must cook at a very low temperature.

> 4 egg whites
> 225 g/8 oz granulated sugar
> 20 ml/1 tbsp malt vinegar
> pinch of salt
> 275 ml/½ pt double or whipping cream

Put the egg whites in a bowl and beat until they are really stiff – use an electric beater if you have one. When they are stiff and shiny, add the sugar, a little at a time, then add the vinegar and salt and continue beating until the mixture will hold its shape. I usually prepare the baking tray while my electric beater does all the work.

To prepare the baking tray, thoroughly grease a sheet of tinfoil or greaseproof paper then run it quickly under the cold tap. Shake off the excess water and place the greased sheet on the tray.

Spoon the mixture carefully onto the greased sheet, shaping it into a circle. Remember that it will spread slightly during cooking. Bake at 120°C/250°F/gas mark ¾ for 40 minutes, then turn the oven down to 100°C/200°F/gas mark ½ for a further 20 minutes. (If you have a top and bottom heating oven, turn off the top heat before you start cooking to prevent the cake from going brown on top.) The cake is cooked when it is just brittle to touch. Allow to cool before carefully removing the greased paper.

Cover the cake with the whipped cream and decorate.

SUMMER PAVLOVA

This is a real New Zealand Pav, and I think the taste of passion fruit is one of the best in the world. Make sure that you buy fresh ones, if they are too old and shrivelled there will be hardly any pulp inside.

> 1 meringue base
> 3–4 passion fruit
> 275 ml/½ pt double or whipping cream
> 1 kiwi fruit
> 225 g/8 oz strawberries or raspberries

Whip the cream and then stir in the passion fruit pulp and spread over the meringue base. Peel and thinly slice the kiwi fruit, and arrange in a circle around the edge of the cake. Place the strawberries or raspberries in an attractive pattern in the centre.

WINTER PAVLOVA

The sharpness of the lemon curd makes a nice contrast to the sweetness of the meringue in this version. The recipe also uses up the egg yolks left over from the meringue.

> 1 meringue base
> 4 egg yolks
> 50 g/2 oz caster sugar
> 1 lemon
> 275 ml/½ pt double or whipping cream
> 50 g/2 oz toasted blanched almonds
> Black or green seedless grapes

Finely grate the rind of the lemon. Squeeze the juice from the lemon and set to one side. Put the egg yolks in a bowl and beat slightly before placing the bowl over a pan of gently simmering water. Continue beating until the eggs are thick and light, then add the sugar, lemon zest and lemon juice. Keep stirring and cooking until the mixture becomes thick and shiny.

Allow the mixture to cool before spreading it over the meringue base. Whip the cream, and spread it over the lemon filling. Then decorate with the toasted almonds and grapes.

Viennese Coffee Cake

This is definitely a cake-lovers cake. Make it, and dream yourself away to romantic coffee houses in far-away cities.

110 g/4 oz butter
175 g/6 oz sugar
3 eggs separated
10 g/1 tbsp instant coffee
30 g/3 tbsp hot water
110 g/4 oz sifted flour
10 g/2 tsp baking powder
50 g/2 oz ground pistachio nuts
Apricot glaze (page 41)

Decoration
110 g/4 oz chopped pistachio nuts
Chocolate leaves (page 46)

Chocolate filling
110 g/4 oz unsalted butter
110 g/4 oz icing sugar
110 g/4 oz plain chocolate
25 g/2 tbsp liqueur (optional)

Chantilly cream
137 ml/¼ pt double cream
15 g/3 tsp icing sugar
Few drops of vanilla essence

Cream the butter and sugar together. Add 1 tsp of flour and the yolk of one egg and beat well; repeat twice and then continue beating until the mixture is light and creamy. Add half of the flour and fold in. Dissolve the coffee essence in the hot water and add it to the egg and flour. Then fold in the rest of the flour, the baking powder and the ground nuts. Mix gently to combine.

Beat the egg whites until they are stiff, then fold them into the cake mixture, making sure there is not a well of liquid in the bottom of the bowl.

Thoroughly grease and lightly dust with flour a 450 g/1 lb loaf tin. Put the cake mixture into the tin and bake at 190°C/375°F/gas mark 5 for 35–40 minutes. When cooked, remove it from the tin and cool on a wire rack.

To make the chocolate filling, melt the chocolate in a bowl over a small pan of simmering water. In another bowl, beat the butter and sugar until the mixture is pale and creamy. Pour in the melted chocolate, add the liqueur, mix and leave to cool.

To make the Chantilly cream, beat the cream until it will just hold its shape, then gently beat in the icing sugar and the vanilla essence.

Using a large sharp knife, carefully slice the cake horizontally into three. Spread half of the chocolate filling on each of the two lower layers and sandwich the cake back together. Using a pastry brush, cover the sides and ends of the cake with apricot glaze. Spread the chopped pistachio nuts on a flat surface and, holding the cake carefully, press each end and both sides into the nuts so that the nuts stick to the glaze.

Spread the chantilly cream over the top of the cake, and smooth it with a palette knife. Then use an icing bag to pipe the other half in an attractive design and decorate with chocolate leaves. As a finishing touch you could sift a fine sprinkling of cocoa over the cream.

Novelty Cakes

Basic Victoria Sponge

I have used a Victoria sponge as the base for all the novelty cakes in this chapter, but you could use almost any cake recipe. For example the snowman (this page) could be made using a fruit cake base, but you would have to alter the cooking times. The Victoria sponge is an easily adaptable cake; keeping the basic proportions of eggs to butter, sugar and flour constant, you can make a cake as big or as small as you like. For example, a 4-egg cake (twice the number of eggs in the recipe) would need twice the amount of all the other ingredients (220 g/8 oz butter, 220 g/8 oz sugar, 220 g/8 oz self-raising flour).

2 eggs
110 g/4 oz butter
110 g/4 oz sugar
110 g/ 4 oz self-raising flour
Flavouring (see below)

Cream the butter and sugar until they are light and fluffy. Add the eggs one at a time, each with a teaspoon of flour, and continue beating. When the mixture is well blended, fold in the rest of the flour.

Bake in a well greased tin at 180°C/375°F/gas mark 4. See individual cakes for cooking times.

Chocolate flavoured sponge
Add 40 g/1 rounded tbsp of cocoa and a few drops of vanilla essence to the sifted flour.

Lemon or orange flavoured sponge
Add the grated rind and the juice of half a lemon or orange before folding in the flour.

Coffee flavoured sponge
Add 10 g/1 tbsp of instant coffee dissolved in an equal amount of hot water before folding in the flour.

Christmas Snowman

YOU WILL NEED:

4-egg Victoria sponge mixture (page 73)
Ovenproof pudding basin of ½ l/1 pt capacity
Ovenproof pudding basin of 1 1/2 pt capacity
675 g/1½ lb moulding icing (page 52)
Black paste colouring
Pontefract cakes (or liquorice circles)
Orange peel
Ribbon

Thoroughly grease and lightly dust with flour the pudding basins. Mix up the 4-egg sponge mixture. Place two thirds in the large bowl and one third in the small bowl. Bake at the proper temperature, allowing approximately 45 minutes for the smaller cake and 1 hour for the larger cake. Test with a thin skewer to make sure the cake is cooked right through. If the top of the cake is in danger of overcooking before the cake is completely cooked, place a piece of tinfoil lightly over the bowl.

After the cakes have cooked, turn them out onto a wire rack to cool. I suggest you loosen the sides of the cakes gently with a palette knife.

When both the cakes are cold, brush them with apricot glaze.

Roll out one third of the moulding icing for the small cake and two thirds for the large cake. Cover the cakes with icing. Spread more apricot glaze over the top of the large cake to hold the small cake in place, and glue the two parts together.

Colour the trimmings from the moulding icing black. Roll out and cut into two circles, one slightly larger than the other. Put the smaller circle on top of the larger one to make a black hat.

Cut two Pontefract or pieces of liquorice cakes to make the snowman's eyes. Cut out a piece of orange peel for the mouth, another piece for the nose and two pieces for the eyebrows. Put two Pontefract cakes or liquorice circles down the front of the big cake for buttons.

When the icing is dry tie a piece of ribbon round the snowman's neck.

Hallowe'en Cake

YOU WILL NEED:

5-egg Victoria sponge mixture (page 73)
800 g/1½ lb moulding icing
Two ovenproof pudding basins of ½ l/1 pt capacity
Orange, black, yellow and green food colouring
1 flake chocolate bar

Make up the 5-egg sponge mixture and divide it evenly into the well greased pudding basins. Bake at the correct temperature for approximately 1 hour. Check with a thin metal skewer to make sure the cakes are properly cooked. When they are cooked, loosen the sides with a palette knife to ensure that they come out whole. Cool on a wire rack.

When the cakes are cool, join them together with apricot glaze to make a pumpkin shape.

Make templates of witches, bats and moons (see page 42).

Colour a small piece of the moulding icing yellow to make the moons, another small piece green to make leaves, then a larger piece black to make the witches and bats. Colour the rest orange and roll out to cover the cake. Wrap the edges under the cake, then use the handle of a small paint brush or a similar object to make indentations down the side of the cake to represent the lines on the pumpkin.

Place the witches, bats and moons on the cake. Cut a piece of the flake bar to represent the stalk of the pumpkin; put it on top of the cake and hold it in place with leaves made from the green icing.

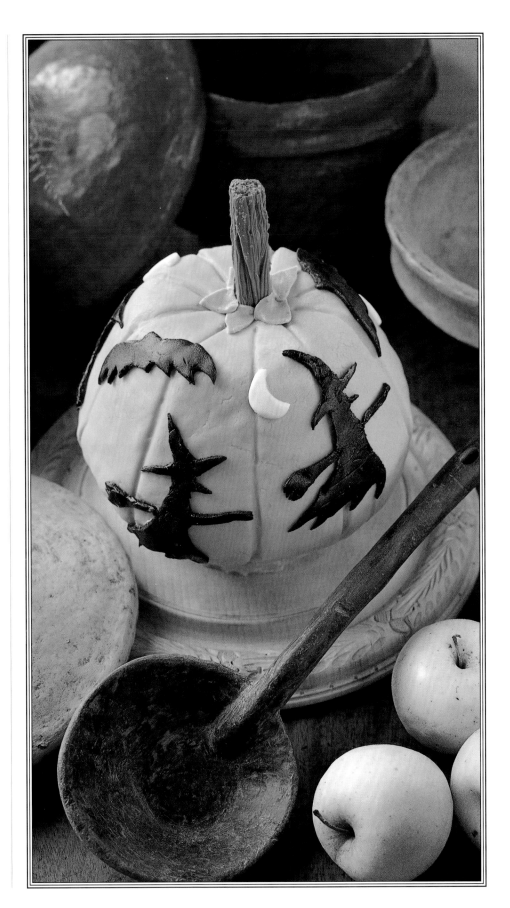

Magic Garden

YOU WILL NEED:

4-egg Victoria sponge mixture (page 73)

50 g/2 oz desiccated coconut

Green food colouring

225 g/½ lb Glacé icing (page 27)

Broken biscuits

Moulding icing and/or almond paste to make into birds, flowers, leaves, butterflies and a hedgehog (page 50)

A small mirror or small piece of tinfoil

A small branching twig

Make up the 4-egg sponge mixture. Bake in a well greased or lined 23cm/ 9 in round cake tin at the correct temperature for 1–1½ hours. When cooked, turn out onto a wire rack to cool. Place the cake on a flat plate or cake board ready to ice.

To make the tree, secure the branching twig into a piece of almond paste. Make up a small quantity of runny glacé icing, then use a teaspoon to drip the icing all over the branch. Leave for a short time to dry and then drip another layer on. When the branch is completely covered, leave to dry off properly and then paint with green food colouring. When the paint is dry, stick on the leaves using glacé icing.

To colour the desiccated coconut, spread it out on a piece of tinfoil, sprinkle liberally with food colouring and then mix the colouring through the coconut until all the strands are coloured. Colour ¾ of it green and ¼ brown.

Make up the rest of the glacé icing and colour it green. Spread roughly over the cake and sprinkle with the green desiccated coconut before the icing dries.

Place the mirror and the tree on the cake. You may need to secure them with moulding icing or almond paste. Disguise the edge of the pond and the base of the tree with green icing and broken biscuits.

Make the hedgehog out of moulding icing or almond paste and cover it with the brown desiccated coconut.

Arrange the birds, flowers, butterflies and hedgehog in the garden.

American Football Cake

The proportions of an American Football field are slightly over twice as long as it is wide. For the purposes of a cake we can cheat a bit and make a cake in 2 square tins to be joined together to form an oblong shape.

YOU WILL NEED:

6-egg Victoria sponge mixture (page 73)

450 g/1 lb glacé (page 27) or fondant (page 33)
icing

Desiccated coconut

Piece of thick card 45.5cm/18in long × 23cm/9in wide

Tinfoil to cover card

Green and red food colouring

8 straws

2 pieces liquorice tube

Miniature football figures, bought or modelled from almond paste

A miniature football, bought or modelled from almond paste.

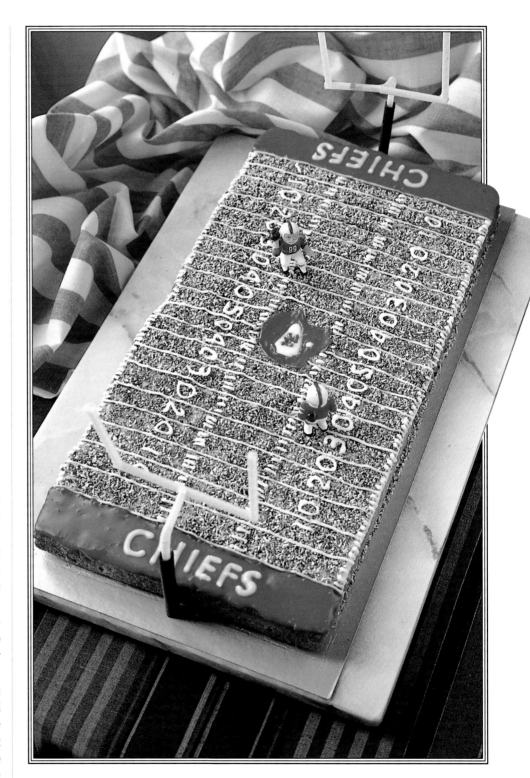

Make up the 6-egg sponge mixture and bake it in two 23cm/9 in square well greased cake tins at the proper temperature for 1½ hours. If you only have one correctly sized tin, cook two separate 3-egg mixtures. Turn out to cool on a wire rack.

Cover the sheet of card with the tinfoil and place the cakes on it, end to end. Join the cakes together with jam or icing.

In an eggcup, mix up some green food colouring with a few drops of red added to make a good grass colour. Use to colour most of the glacé or fondant icing and the desiccated coconut. Leave a small amount of icing white to mark out the lines and numbers on the football field, and colour enough red (or another colour) to use for either end of the field.

Ice the cake appropriately in the green and red icing. Cover the green icing with the desiccated coconut before putting the colour on the ends.

Pipe the lines and numbers on using a thin nozzle.

Make the goal posts out of the straws using small blobs of icing to stick them together. Use the liquorice tubes to stand the goal posts in. Place the goal posts, the ball and the figures on the field.

Index

T

V

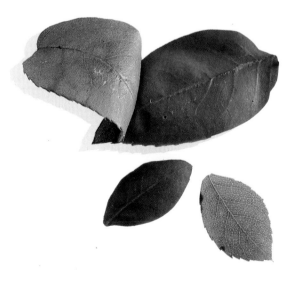